The Key Facts™

on

Italy

Essential Information on Italy

By Patrick W. Nee

The Internationalist®

www.internationalist.com

The Internationalist®

International Business, Investment, and Travel

Published by:

The Internationalist Publishing Company

96 Walter Street/ Suite 200

Boston, MA 02131, USA

Tel: 617-354-7722

www.internationalist.com

PN@internationalist.com

Table Of Contents

Chapter 1: Background

Chapter 2: Geography

Chapter 3: People and Society

Chapter 4: Government and Key Leaders

Chapter 5: Economy

Chapter 6: Energy

Chapter 7: Communications

Chapter 8: Transportation

Chapter 9: Military

Chapter 10: Transnational Issues

Chapter 1: Background

Italy became a nation-state in 1861 when the regional states of the peninsula, along with Sardinia and Sicily, were united under King Victor EMMANUEL II. An era of parliamentary government came to a close in the early 1920s when Benito MUSSOLINI established a Fascist dictatorship. His alliance with Nazi Germany led to Italy's defeat in World War II. A democratic republic replaced the monarchy in 1946 and economic revival followed. Italy is a charter member of NATO and the European Economic Community (EEC). It has been at the forefront of European economic and political unification, joining the Economic and Monetary Union in 1999. Persistent problems include sluggish economic growth, low youth and female employment, organized crime, corruption, and economic disparities between southern Italy and the more prosperous north.

Chapter 2: Geography

Location:

> Southern Europe, a peninsula extending into the central Mediterranean Sea, northeast of Tunisia

Geographic coordinates:

> 42 50 N, 12 50 E

Map references:

> Europe

Area:

> total: 301,340 sq km
>
> country comparison to the world: 72
>
> land: 294,140 sq km
>
> water: 7,200 sq km
>
> note: includes Sardinia and Sicily

Area - comparative:

> slightly larger than Arizona

Land boundaries:

> total: 1,899.2 km
>
> border countries: Austria 430 km, France 488 km, Holy See (Vatican City) 3.2 km, San Marino 39 km, Slovenia 199 km, Switzerland 740 km

Coastline:

> 7,600 km

Maritime claims:

> territorial sea: 12 nm

continental shelf: 200 m depth or to the depth of
exploitation

Climate:

predominantly Mediterranean; Alpine in far north; hot, dry
in south

Terrain:

mostly rugged and mountainous; some plains, coastal
lowlands

Elevation extremes:

lowest point: Mediterranean Sea 0 m

highest point: Mont Blanc (Monte Bianco) de Courmayeur
4,748 m (a secondary peak of Mont Blanc)

Natural resources:

coal, mercury, zinc, potash, marble, barite, asbestos,
pumice, fluorspar, feldspar, pyrite (sulfur), natural gas and
crude oil reserves, fish, arable land

Land use:

arable land: 26.41%

permanent crops: 9.09%

other: 64.5% (2005)

Irrigated land:

39,500 sq km (2003)

Total renewable water resources:

175 cu km (2005)

Freshwater withdrawal (domestic/industrial/agricultural):

total: 41.98 cu km/yr (18%/37%/45%)

Natural hazards:

regional risks include landslides, mudflows, avalanches, earthquakes, volcanic eruptions, flooding; land subsidence in Venice

volcanism: significant volcanic activity; Etna (elev. 3,330 m), which is in eruption as of 2010, is Europe's most active volcano; flank eruptions pose a threat to nearby Sicilian villages; Etna, along with the famous Vesuvius, which remains a threat to the millions of nearby residents in the Bay of Naples area, have both been deemed "Decade Volcanoes" by the International Association of Volcanology and Chemistry of the Earth's Interior, worthy of study due to their explosive history and close proximity to human populations; Stromboli, on its namesake island, has also been continuously active with moderate volcanic activity; other historically active volcanoes include Campi Flegrei, Ischia, Larderello, Pantelleria, Vulcano, and Vulsini

Environment - current issues:

air pollution from industrial emissions such as sulfur dioxide; coastal and inland rivers polluted from industrial and agricultural effluents; acid rain damaging lakes; inadequate industrial waste treatment and disposal facilities

Environment - international agreements:

party to: Air Pollution, Air Pollution-Nitrogen Oxides, Air Pollution-Persistent Organic Pollutants, Air Pollution-Sulfur 85, Air Pollution-Sulfur 94, Air Pollution-Volatile Organic Compounds, Antarctic-Environmental Protocol, Antarctic-Marine Living Resources, Antarctic Seals, Antarctic Treaty, Biodiversity, Climate Change, Climate Change-Kyoto Protocol, Desertification, Endangered Species, Environmental Modification, Hazardous Wastes, Law of the Sea, Marine Dumping, Ozone Layer Protection, Ship Pollution, Tropical Timber 83, Tropical Timber 94, Wetlands, Whaling

signed, but not ratified: none of the selected agreements

Geography - note:

strategic location dominating central Mediterranean as well as southern sea and air approaches to Western Europe

Chapter 3: People and Society

Nationality:

noun: Italian(s)

adjective: Italian

Ethnic groups:

Italian (includes small clusters of German-, French-, and Slovene-Italians in the north and Albanian-Italians and Greek-Italians in the south)

Languages:

Italian (official), German (parts of Trentino-Alto Adige region are predominantly German speaking), French (small French-speaking minority in Valle d'Aosta region), Slovene (Slovene-speaking minority in the Trieste-Gorizia area)

Religions:

Christian 80% (overwhelming Roman Catholic with very small groups of Jehova Witnesses and Protestants), Muslims NEGL (about 700,000 but growing), Atheists and Agnostics 20%

Population:

61,261,254 (July 2012 est.)

country comparison to the world: 23

Age structure:

0-14 years: 13.8% (male 4,327,307/female 4,138,369)

15-24 years: 10% (male 3,071,801/female 3,041,450)

25-54 years: 43.3% (male 13,143,815/female 13,409,511)

55-64 years: 12.4% (male 3,667,498/female 3,904,324)

65 years and over: 20.5% (male 5,350,173/female
7,207,006) (2012 est.)

Median age:

total: 43.8 years

male: 42.7 years

female: 45 years (2012 est.)

Population growth rate:

0.38% (2012 est.)

country comparison to the world: 157

Birth rate:

9.06 births/1,000 population (2012 est.)

country comparison to the world: 208

Death rate:

9.93 deaths/1,000 population (July 2012 est.)

country comparison to the world: 54

Net migration rate:

4.67 migrant(s)/1,000 population (2012 est.)

country comparison to the world: 22

Urbanization:

urban population: 68% of total population (2010)

rate of urbanization: 0.5% annual rate of change (2010-15
est.)

Major cities - population:

ROME (capital) 3.357 million; Milan 2.962 million; Naples 2.27 million; Turin 1.662 million; Palermo 872,000 (2009)

Sex ratio:

at birth: 1.06 male(s)/female

under 15 years: 1.05 male(s)/female

15-64 years: 0.98 male(s)/female

65 years and over: 0.74 male(s)/female

total population: 0.93 male(s)/female (2011 est.)

Maternal mortality rate:

4 deaths/100,000 live births (2010)

country comparison to the world: 180

Infant mortality rate:

total: 3.36 deaths/1,000 live births

country comparison to the world: 215

male: 3.56 deaths/1,000 live births

female: 3.14 deaths/1,000 live births (2012 est.)

Life expectancy at birth:

total population: 81.86 years

country comparison to the world: 10

male: 79.24 years

female: 84.63 years (2012 est.)

Total fertility rate:

1.4 children born/woman (2012 est.)

country comparison to the world: 204

Health expenditures:

5.1% of GDP (2009)

country comparison to the world: 136

Physicians density:

4.242 physicians/1,000 population (2008)

Hospital bed density:

3.7 beds/1,000 population (2008)

HIV/AIDS - adult prevalence rate:

0.3% (2009 est.)

country comparison to the world: 83

HIV/AIDS - people living with HIV/AIDS:

140,000 (2009 est.)

country comparison to the world: 34

HIV/AIDS - deaths:

fewer than 1,000 (2009 est.)

country comparison to the world: 78

Obesity - adult prevalence rate:

9.8% (2005)

country comparison to the world: 56

Education expenditures:

4.3% of GDP (2007)

country comparison to the world: 91

Literacy:

definition: age 15 and over can read and write

total population: 98.4%

male: 98.8%

female: 98% (2001 census)

School life expectancy (primary to tertiary education):

> total: 16 years
>
> male: 16 years
>
> female: 17 years (2008)

Unemployment, youth ages 15-24:

> total: 25.4%
>
> country comparison to the world: 27
>
> male: 23.3%
>
> female: 28.7% (2009)

Chapter 4: Government and Key Leaders

Country name:

conventional long form: Italian Republic

conventional short form: Italy

local long form: Repubblica Italiana

local short form: Italia

former: Kingdom of Italy

Government type:

republic

Capital:

name: Rome

geographic coordinates: 41 54 N, 12 29 E

time difference: UTC+1 (6 hours ahead of Washington, DC during Standard Time)

daylight saving time: +1hr, begins last Sunday in March; ends last Sunday in October

Administrative divisions:

15 regions (regioni, singular - regione) and 5 autonomous regions (regioni autonome, singular - regione autonoma)

regions: Abruzzo, Basilicata, Calabria, Campania, Emilia-Romagna, Lazio (Latium), Liguria, Lombardia, Marche, Molise, Piemonte (Piedmont), Puglia (Apulia), Toscana (Tuscany), Umbria, Veneto (Venetia)

autonomous regions: Friuli-Venezia Giulia; Sardegna (Sardinia); Sicilia (Sicily); Trentino-Alto Adige (Trentino-

South Tyrol) or Trentino-Suedtirol (German); Valle d'Aosta (Aosta Valley) or Vallee d'Aoste (French)

Independence:

17 March 1861 (Kingdom of Italy proclaimed; Italy was not finally unified until 1870)

National holiday:

Republic Day, 2 June (1946)

Constitution:

passed 11 December 1947, effective 1 January 1948; amended many times

Legal system:

civil law system; judicial review under certain conditions in Constitutional Court

International law organization participation:

has not submitted an ICJ jurisdiction declaration; accepts ICCt jurisdiction

Suffrage:

18 years of age; universal (except in senatorial elections, where minimum age is 25)

Executive branch:

chief of state: President Giorgio NAPOLITANO (since 15 May 2006)

head of government: Prime Minister Mario MONTI (since 16 November 2011); note - in Italy the prime minister is referred to as the President of the Council of Ministers; Mario MONTI resigned on 21 December 2012

cabinet: Council of Ministers proposed by the Prime
Minister and nominated by the President of the Republic
elections: president elected by an electoral college
consisting of both houses of parliament and 58 regional
representatives for a seven-year term (no term limits);
election last held on 10 May 2006 (next to be held in May
2013); prime minister appointed by the president and
confirmed by parliament
election results: Giorgio NAPOLITANO elected president
on the fourth round of voting; electoral college vote - 543

Legislative branch:

bicameral Parliament or Parlamento consists of the Senate
or Senato della Repubblica (315 seats; members elected by
proportional vote with the winning coalition in each region
receiving 55% of seats from that region; members to serve
five-year terms; and up to 5 senators for life appointed by
the president of the Republic) and the Chamber of
Deputies or Camera dei Deputati (630 seats; members
elected by popular vote with the winning national coalition
receiving 54% of chamber seats; members to serve five-
year terms); note - it has not been clarified if each
president has the power to designate up to five senators or
if five is the number of senators for life who might sit in
the Senate
elections: Senate - last held on 13-14 April 2008 (next to
be held 24-25 February 2013); Chamber of Deputies - last

held on 13-14 April 2008 (next to be held 24-25 February 2013)

election results: Senate - percent of vote by party - NA; seats by party - S. BERLUSCONI coalition 174 (PdL 147, LN 25, MpA 2), W. VELTRONI coalition 132 (PD 118, IdV 3), UdC 3, other 6; Chamber of Deputies - percent of vote by party - NA; seats by party - S. BERLUSCONI coalition 344 (PdL 276, LN 60, MpA 8), W. VELTRONI coalition 246 (PD 217, IdV 29), UdC 36, other 4; note - President NAPOLITANO dissolved Parliament on 22 December 2012

Judicial branch:

Constitutional Court or Corte Costituzionale (composed of 15 judges: one-third appointed by the president, one-third elected by parliament, one-third elected by the ordinary and administrative Supreme Courts); Supreme Court of Cassation or Corte Suprema di Cassazione

Political parties and leaders:

Center-Right: People of Freedom or PdL [Anelino ALFANO]

Center-Left: Democratic Party or PD [Pier Luigi BERSAN]

Centrist Third Pole: Future and Freedom for Italy or FLI [Gianfranco FINI]; Movement for Autonomy or MpA [Raffaele LOMBARDO]; Union of the Center or UdC [Pier Ferdinando CASINI]

no affiliation: Italy of Values or IdV [Antonio DI PIETRO]; Lega Nord or LN [Roberto MARONI]; Five Star Movment or M5S [Beppe GRILLO]

Political pressure groups and leaders:

manufacturers and merchants associations - Confcommercio; Confindustria; organized farm groups - Confcoltivatori; Confagricoltura; Roman Catholic Church; three major trade union confederations - Confederazione Generale Italiana del Lavoro or CGIL [Susanna CAMUSSO] which is left wing; Confederazione Italiana dei Sindacati Lavoratori or CISL [Raffaele BONANNI], which is Roman Catholic centrist; Unione Italiana del Lavoro or UIL [Luigi ANGELETTI] which is lay centrist

International organization participation:

ADB (nonregional member), AfDB (nonregional member), Australia Group, BIS, BSEC (observer), CBSS (observer), CD, CDB, CE, CEI, CERN, EAPC, EBRD, ECB, EIB, EITI (implementing country), EMU, ESA, EU, FAO, FATF, G-20, G-7, G-8, G-10, IADB, IAEA, IBRD, ICAO, ICC (national committees), ICRM, IDA, IEA, IFAD, IFC, IFRCS, IGAD (partners), IHO, ILO, IMF, IMO, IMSO, Interpol, IOC, IOM, IPU, ISO, ITSO, ITU, ITUC (NGOs), LAIA (observer), MIGA, MINURSO, NATO, NEA, NSG, OAS (observer), OECD, OPCW, OSCE, Paris Club, PCA, PIF (partner), Schengen Convention, SELEC (observer), SICA (observer), UN,

UNAMID, UNCTAD, UNESCO, UNHCR, UNIDO, UNIFIL, Union Latina, UNMISS, UNMOGIP, UNRWA, UNTSO, UNWTO, UPU, WCO, WHO, WIPO, WMO, WTO, ZC

Diplomatic representation in the US:

chief of mission: Ambassador Claudio BISOGNIERO

chancery: 3000 Whitehaven Street NW, Washington, DC 20008

telephone: [1] (202) 612-4400

FAX: [1] (202) 518-2151

consulate(s) general: Boston, Chicago, Houston, Miami, New York, Los Angeles, Philadelphia, San Francisco

consulate(s): Detroit

Diplomatic representation from the US:

chief of mission: Ambassador David THORNE

embassy: Via Vittorio Veneto 121, 00187-Rome

mailing address: PSC 59, Box 100, APO AE 09624

telephone: [39] (06) 46741

FAX: [39] (06) 488-2672, 4674-2356

consulate(s) general: Florence, Milan, Naples

Key Leaders:

Pres.	Giorgio NAPOLITANO
Prime Min.	Mario MONTI
Under Sec. for the Presidency of the Council of Ministers	Antonio CATRICALA
Min. of Agriculture	Mario CATANIA

Min. of Community Policy	Enzo Moavero MILANESI
Min. of Cultural Assets	Lorenzo ORNAGHI
Min. of Defense	Giampaolo DI PAOLA
Min. of Economic Development	Corrado PASSERA
Min. of Economy & Finance	Vittorio GRILLI
Min. of Education	Franceso PROFUMO
Min. of Environment	Corrado CLINI
Min. of Foreign Affairs	Giulio TERZI di Sant' Agata
Min. of Health	Renato BALDUZZI
Min. of Infrastructure & Transport	Corrado PASSERA
Min. of Interior	Anna Maria CANCELLIERI
Min. of Intl. Cooperation	Andrea RICCARDI
Min. of Justice	Paola SEVERINO
Min. of Labor, Welfare, & Equal Opportunity	Elsa FORNERO
Min. of Relations With Parliament	Piero GIARDA
Min. of Territorial Cohesion	Fabrizio BARCA
Min. of Tourism & Sport	Piero GNUDI
Governor, Bank of Italy	Ignazio VISCO
Ambassador to the US	Claudio BISOGNIERO

Permanent Representative to the UN, New York	Cesare Maria RAGAGLINI

Flag description:

three equal vertical bands of green (hoist side), white, and red; design inspired by the French flag brought to Italy by Napoleon in 1797; colors are those of Milan (red and white) combined with the green uniform color of the Milanese civic guard

note: similar to the flag of Mexico, which is longer, uses darker shades of red and green, and has its coat of arms centered on the white band; Ireland, which is longer and is green (hoist side), white, and orange; also similar to the flag of the Cote d'Ivoire, which has the colors reversed - orange (hoist side), white, and green

National symbol(s):

white, five-pointed star (Stella d'Italia)

National anthem:

name: "Il Canto degli Italiani" (The Song of the Italians)

lyrics/music: Goffredo MAMELI/Michele NOVARO

note: adopted 1946; the anthem, originally written in 1847, is also known as "L'Inno di Mameli" (Mameli's Hymn), and "Fratelli D'Italia" (Brothers of Italy)

Chapter 5: Economy

Economy - overview:

Italy has a diversified industrial economy, which is divided into a developed industrial north, dominated by private companies, and a less-developed, highly subsidized, agricultural south, with high unemployment. The Italian economy is driven in large part by the manufacture of high-quality consumer goods produced by small and medium-sized enterprises, many of them family owned. Italy also has a sizable underground economy, which by some estimates accounts for as much as 17% of GDP. These activities are most common within the agriculture, construction, and service sectors. Italy is the third-largest economy in the euro-zone, but its exceptionally high public debt and structural impediments to growth have rendered it vulnerable to scrutiny by financial markets. Public debt has increased steadily since 2007, topping 126% of GDP in 2012, and investor concerns about the broader euro-zone crisis at times have caused borrowing costs on sovereign government debt to rise to euro-era records. During the second half of 2011 the government passed a series of three austerity packages to balance its budget and decrease its public debt. These measures included a hike in the value-added tax, pension reforms, and cuts to public administration. The government also faces pressure from investors and European partners to sustain its recent efforts to address Italy's long-standing structural impediments to growth, such as an inflexible labor market and widespread tax evasion. In 2012 economic growth and labor market conditions deteriorated, with growth at -2.3% and unemployment rising to nearly 11%. Although the government has undertaken several economic reform iniatiatives, in the longer-term Italy's low fertility rate, productivity, and foreign investment will increasingly strain its economy. Italy's GDP is now 7% below its 2007 pre-crisis level.

GDP (purchasing power parity):

$1.834 trillion (2012 est.)

country comparison to the world: 11

$1.877 trillion (2011 est.)

$1.869 trillion (2010 est.)

note: data are in 2012 US dollars

GDP (official exchange rate):

$1.98 trillion (2012 est.)

GDP - real growth rate:

-2.3% (2012 est.)

country comparison to the world: 207

0.4% (2011 est.)

1.8% (2010 est.)

GDP - per capita (PPP):

$30,100 (2012 est.)

country comparison to the world: 45

$31,000 (2011 est.)

$31,000 (2010 est.)

note: data are in 2012 US dollars

GDP - composition by sector:

agriculture: 2%

industry: 23.9%

services: 74.1% (2012 est.)

Labor force:

25.28 million (2012 est.)

country comparison to the world: 25

Labor force - by occupation:

agriculture: 3.9%

industry: 28.3%

services: 67.8% (2011)

Unemployment rate:

10.9% (2012 est.)

country comparison to the world: 117

8.4% (2011 est.)

Household income or consumption by percentage share:

lowest 10%: 2.3%

highest 10%: 26.8% (2000)

Distribution of family income - Gini index:

31.9 (2011)

country comparison to the world: 106

27.3 (1995)

Investment (gross fixed):

18.2% of GDP (2012 est.)

country comparison to the world: 118

Budget:

revenues: $956.6 billion

expenditures: $1.014 trillion (2012 est.)

Taxes and other revenues:

48.3% of GDP (2012 est.)

country comparison to the world: 23

Budget surplus (+) or deficit (-):

-2.9% of GDP (2012 est.)

country comparison to the world: 105

Public debt:

126.1% of GDP (2012 est.)

country comparison to the world: 8

120.1% of GDP (2011 est.)

note: Italy reports its data on public debt according to guidelines set out in the Maastricht Treaty; general government gross debt is defined in the Maastricht Treaty as consolidated general government gross debt at nominal value, outstanding at the end of the year, in the following categories of government liabilities (as defined in ESA95): currency and deposits (AF.2), securities other than shares excluding financial derivatives (AF.3, excluding AF.34), and loans (AF.4); the general government sector comprises

the central government, state government, local
government and social security funds

Inflation rate (consumer prices):

3% (2012 est.)

country comparison to the world: 78

2.9% (2011 est.)

Central bank discount rate:

1.5% (31 December 2012)

country comparison to the world: 115

1.75% (31 December 2010)

note: this is the European Central Bank's rate on the
marginal lending facility, which offers overnight credit to
banks in the euro area

Commercial bank prime lending rate:

4.2% (31 December 2012 est.)

country comparison to the world: 162

4.6% (31 December 2011 est.)

Stock of narrow money:

$1.137 trillion (31 December 2012 est.)

country comparison to the world: 6

$1.147 trillion (31 December 2011 est.)

note: see entry for the European Union for money supply
in the euro area; the European Central Bank (ECB)
controls monetary policy for the 17 members of the
Economic and Monetary Union (EMU); individual

members of the EMU do not control the quantity of money circulating within their own borders

Stock of broad money:

$1.944 trillion (31 December 2012 est.)

country comparison to the world: 10

$1.957 trillion (31 December 2011 est.)

Stock of domestic credit:

$3.122 trillion (31 December 2012 est.)

country comparison to the world: 8

$3.209 trillion (31 December 2011 est.)

Market value of publicly traded shares:

$431.5 billion (31 December 2011)

country comparison to the world: 27

$318.1 billion (31 December 2010)

$317.3 billion (31 December 2009)

Agriculture - products:

fruits, vegetables, grapes, potatoes, sugar beets, soybeans, grain, olives; beef, dairy products; fish

Industries:

tourism, machinery, iron and steel, chemicals, food processing, textiles, motor vehicles, clothing, footwear, ceramics

Industrial production growth rate:

0.2% (2011 est.)

country comparison to the world: 147

Current account balance:

-$30.3 billion (2012 est.)

country comparison to the world: 184

-$71.87 billion (2011 est.)

Exports:

$483.3 billion (2012 est.)

country comparison to the world: 10

$524.9 billion (2011 est.)

Exports - commodities:

engineering products, textiles and clothing, production
machinery, motor vehicles, transport equipment,
chemicals; food, beverages and tobacco; minerals, and
nonferrous metals

Exports - partners:

Germany 13.3%, France 11.8%, US 5.9%, Spain 5.4%,
Switzerland 5.4%, UK 4.7% (2011)

Imports:

$469.7 billion (2012 est.)

country comparison to the world: 13

$549.6 billion (2011 est.)

Imports - commodities:

engineering products, chemicals, transport equipment,
energy products, minerals and nonferrous metals, textiles
and clothing; food, beverages, and tobacco

Imports - partners:

Germany 16.5%, France 8.8%, China 7.7%, Netherlands
5.5%, Spain 4.7% (2011)

Reserves of foreign exchange and gold:

$173.3 billion (31 December 2011 est.)

country comparison to the world: 14

$158.9 billion (2010 est.)

Debt - external:

$2.46 trillion (30 June 2012 est.)

country comparison to the world: 9

$2.684 trillion (30 June 2011 est.)

Stock of direct foreign investment - at home:

$369.5 billion (31 December 2012 est.)

country comparison to the world: 16

$338.5 billion (31 December 2011 est.)

Stock of direct foreign investment - abroad:

$537 billion (31 December 2012 est.)

country comparison to the world: 12

$492.2 billion (31 December 2011 est.)

Exchange rates:

euros (EUR) per US dollar -

0.7838 (2012 est.)

0.7185 (2011 est.)

0.755 (2010 est.)

0.7198 (2009 est.)

0.6827 (2008 est.)

Fiscal year:

calendar year

Chapter 6: Energy

Electricity - production:

302.6 billion kWh (2011 est.)

country comparison to the world: 14

Electricity - consumption:

313.8 billion kWh (2011 est.)

country comparison to the world: 14

Electricity - exports:

1.787 billion kWh (2011 est.)

country comparison to the world: 49

Electricity - imports:

47.52 billion kWh (2011 est.)

country comparison to the world: 3

Electricity - installed generating capacity:

122.3 million kW (2011 est.)

country comparison to the world: 9

Electricity - from fossil fuels:

65% of total installed capacity (2011 est.)

country comparison to the world: 129

Electricity - from nuclear fuels:

0% of total installed capacity (2011 est.)

country comparison to the world: 112

Electricity - from hydroelectric plants:

18% of total installed capacity (2011 est.)

country comparison to the world: 98

Electricity - from other renewable sources:

15.8% of total installed capacity (2011 est.)

country comparison to the world: 10

Crude oil - production:

99,200 bbl/day (2011 est.)

country comparison to the world: 49

Crude oil - exports:

6,300 bbl/day (2010 est.)

country comparison to the world: 59

Crude oil - imports:

1.591 million bbl/day (2010 est.)

country comparison to the world: 8

Crude oil - proved reserves:

523.2 million bbl (1 January 2012 est.)

country comparison to the world: 51

Refined petroleum products - production:

1.887 million bbl/day (2010 est.)

country comparison to the world: 13

Refined petroleum products - consumption:

1.454 million bbl/day (2011 est.)

country comparison to the world: 17

Refined petroleum products - exports:

628,000 bbl/day (2010 est.)

country comparison to the world: 11

Refined petroleum products - imports:

393,300 bbl/day (2010 est.)

country comparison to the world: 15

Natural gas - production:

8.364 billion cu m (2011 est.)

country comparison to the world: 47

Natural gas - consumption:

77.83 billion cu m (2011 est.)

country comparison to the world: 12

Natural gas - exports:

123 million cu m (2011 est.)

country comparison to the world: 46

Natural gas - imports:

70.37 billion cu m (2011 est.)

country comparison to the world: 6

Natural gas - proved reserves:

66 billion cu m (1 January 2012 est.)

country comparison to the world: 61

Carbon dioxide emissions from consumption of energy:

416.4 million Mt (2010 est.)

country comparison to the world: 16

Chapter 7: Communications

Telephones - main lines in use:

22.116 million (2011)

country comparison to the world: 13

Telephones - mobile cellular:

96.005 million (2011)

country comparison to the world: 11

Telephone system:

general assessment: modern, well developed, fast; fully automated telephone, telex, and data services

domestic: high-capacity cable and microwave radio relay trunks

international: country code - 39; a series of submarine cables provide links to Asia, Middle East, Europe, North Africa, and US; satellite earth stations - 3 Intelsat (with a total of 5 antennas - 3 for Atlantic Ocean and 2 for Indian Ocean), 1 Inmarsat (Atlantic Ocean region), and NA Eutelsat

Broadcast media:

two Italian media giants dominate - the publicly-owned Radiotelevisione Italiana (RAI) with 3 national terrestrial stations and privately-owned Mediaset with 3 national terrestrial stations; a large number of private stations and Sky Italia - a satellite TV network; RAI operates 3

AM/FM nationwide radio stations; some 1,300 commercial radio stations (2007)

Internet country code:

.it

Internet hosts:

25.662 million (2012)

country comparison to the world: 4

Internet users:

29.235 million (2009)

country comparison to the world: 13

Chapter 8: Transportation

Airports:

> 130 (2012)

> country comparison to the world: 43

Airports - with paved runways:

> total: 99

> over 3,047 m: 9

> 2,438 to 3,047 m: 31

> 1,524 to 2,437 m: 18

> 914 to 1,523 m: 29

> under 914 m: 12 (2012)

Airports - with unpaved runways:

> total: 31

> 1,524 to 2,437 m: 1

> 914 to 1,523 m: 11

> under 914 m: 19 (2012)

Heliports:

> 5 (2012)

Pipelines:

> gas 18,348 km; oil 1,241 km (2010)

Railways:

> total: 20,255 km

> country comparison to the world: 13

> standard gauge: 18,611 km 1.435-m gauge (12,662 km electrified)

narrow gauge: 123 km 1.000-m gauge (123 km electrified); 1,290 km 0.950-m gauge (151 km electrified); 231 km 0.850-m gauge (2008)

Roadways:

total: 487,700 km

country comparison to the world: 13

paved: 487,700 km (includes 6,700 km of expressways) (2007)

Waterways:

2,400 km (used for commercial traffic; of limited overall value compared to road and rail) (2012)

country comparison to the world: 37

Merchant marine:

total: 681

country comparison to the world: 17

by type: bulk carrier 105, cargo 42, carrier 1, chemical tanker 164, container 21, liquefied gas 28, passenger 25, passenger/cargo 154, petroleum tanker 59, refrigerated cargo 4, roll on/roll off 39, specialized tanker 9, vehicle carrier 30

foreign-owned: 90 (Denmark 4, France 2, Greece 7, Luxembourg 14, Netherlands 2, Nigeria 1, Norway 6, Singapore 1, Sweden 1, Switzerland 13, Taiwan 10, Turkey 4, UK 2, US 23)

registered in other countries: 201 (Bahamas 1, Belize 3, Cayman Islands 7, Cyprus 6, Georgia 2, Gibraltar 4,

Greece 5, Liberia 47, Malta 45, Marshall Islands 1,
Morocco 1, Netherlands 6, Panama 25, Portugal 12, Russia
14, Saint Vincent and the Grenadines 4, Singapore 5,
Slovakia 2, Spain 1, Sweden 5, Turkey 1, UK 3, unknown
1) (2010)

Ports and terminals:

Augusta, Cagliari, Genoa, Livorno, Taranto, Trieste,
Venice

oil terminals: Melilli (Santa Panagia) oil terminal, Sarroch
oil terminal

Chapter 9: Military

Military branches:

Italian Armed Forces: Army (Esercito Italiano, EI), Navy (Marina Militare Italiana, MMI), Italian Air Force (Aeronautica Militare Italiana, AMI), Carabinieri Corps (Arma dei Carabinieri, CC) (2011)

Military service age and obligation:

18-27 year of age for voluntary military service; conscription abolished January 2005; women may serve in any military branch; 10-month service obligation, with a reserve obligation to age 45 (Army and Air Force) or 39 (Navy) (2006)

Manpower available for military service:

males age 16-49: 13,865,688

females age 16-49: 14,003,755 (2010 est.)

Manpower fit for military service:

males age 16-49: 11,247,446

females age 16-49: 11,348,695 (2010 est.)

Manpower reaching militarily significant age annually:

male: 288,188

female: 281,671 (2010 est.)

Military expenditures:

1.8% of GDP (2005 est.)

country comparison to the world: 82

Chapter 10: Transnational Issues

Disputes - international:

Italy's long coastline and developed economy entices tens of thousands of illegal immigrants from southeastern Europe and northern Africa

Illicit drugs:

important gateway for and consumer of Latin American cocaine and Southwest Asian heroin entering the European market; money laundering by organized crime and from smuggling

Other Key Facts™ Titles

Key Facts on Syria

Key Facts on China

Key Facts on Qatar

Key Facts on India

Key Facts on Germany

Key Facts on Argentina

Key Facts on Russia

Key Facts on North Korea

Key Facts on Brazil

Key Facts on Italy

Key Facts on the United Arab Emirates

Key Facts on the European Union

Key Facts on Pakistan

Key Facts on Saudi Arabia

Key Facts on Cyprus

Key Facts on Iran

Key Facts on Afghanistan

Key Facts on Iraq

Key Facts on Indonesia

Key Facts on South Korea

All Key Facts™ Titles are

THE INTERNATIONALIST®

2013

www.internationalist.com